# "A Sentimental Journey"

Elizabeth J. Shupe

outskirtspress
DENVER, COLORADO

The opinions expressed in this manuscript are solely the opinions of the author and do not represent the opinions or thoughts of the publisher. The author has represented and warranted full ownership and/or legal right to publish all the materials in this book.

A Sentimental Journey
All Rights Reserved.
Copyright © 2012 Elizabeth J. Shupe
V2.0

Cover Photo © 2012 Elizabeth J. Shupe. All rights reserved - used with permission.

This book may not be reproduced, transmitted, or stored in whole or in part by any means, including graphic, electronic, or mechanical without the express written consent of the publisher except in the case of brief quotations embodied in critical articles and reviews.

Outskirts Press, Inc.
http://www.outskirtspress.com

ISBN: 978-1-4327-9742-3

Outskirts Press and the "OP" logo are trademarks belonging to Outskirts Press, Inc.

PRINTED IN THE UNITED STATES OF AMERICA

## *Table of Contents*

Chapter 1: "A Baby Girl Was Born" ................................. 1

Chapter 2: "My family, and the world changed" ............... 7

Chapter 3: "From the frying pan, into the fire" ............... 13

Chapter 4: "Unexpected Changes" ................................. 21

Chapter 5: "Life and death experiences" .......................... 27

Chapter 6: "Turning (70) and going strong" ..................... 31

Chapter 7: "Retiring Alive at (75)" ................................. 35

Chapter 8: "Slowing Down, But Not Stopping" ............... 47

During my eight decades, I have had many ups and downs. I thank the Lord for the ability and mindset he has given me to compose my memoirs from eighty years of trials, triumphs, and simple pleasures. Like myself, this book isn't perfect, but I can honestly say that in my lifetime, I have really "lived". I pray it brings encouragement, inspiration, and some laughter to all who read it.

Elizabeth J. Shupe

Pictured (above right) is Ms. Barbara Brown. Pictured (left) are Elizabeth Joanne Shupe and Joyce Grills. This picture was taken at the Haggle Shop in downtown, Kingsport during Christmas of 2011.

# Foreword

I met Elizabeth Joanne Shupe while campaigning for her son, Jantry, for Kingsport City Alderman, on the BMA. From that day forward in 2002, we shared many good times and experiences together. Mrs. Shupe broke her ankle in June, 2009. I stayed at Indian Path Hospital for two weeks with her. Her "healing process" was problematic and required a lot of patience and caring. I told her, one time, that she reminds me of Elizabeth Taylor. She takes great pride in her appearance. As an actress, she has the ability to conceal all of her emotions and smile as if "all is right with the world". Mrs. Shupe entered the hospital again after her 80$^{th}$ birthday.

Once again, Jantry and I transported her to the hospital. This time she had pneumonia, and other problems, that were life-threatening. It was fortunate we got her there just in time. At the present time, she uses a wheelchair, walker and a scooter which she calls her "toy". Her courage and determination astound us! She still has that "Elizabeth Taylor" smile!

Sincerely,<br>
Barbara Brown

# "A Baby Girl Was Born"
## Chapter 1

February 11, 1932, a baby girl was born in Russell County, Virginia, into an humble family. I was the first of five children born during the depression days, beginning my life's journey learning to "make do on less". Our food supply came from our land, growing garden vegetables and canning them for the winter. We raised our own chickens, gathered eggs, milked our cows, and used a crockery churn to churn buttermilk, skimming off the top for butter. We raised hogs for ham, bacon and sausage all year. I hated the process of killing animals such as ringing the chicken's necks, and scraping the hair off hogs and shooting them. It was our way of life to provide food for the family.

We raised turkeys in the country. They had a habit of wandering off when they became frightened by a storm. Our parents would have us go fetch them from the "dark hollow" on the far side of the farm. Our dog, "Fido", was a black and white collie, who played with us and helped us with our chore of bringing them home. My dad gave me a live turkey once to prepare for Thanksgiving. I didn't have the heart to kill it, so dad had to do it for me. I just couldn't stand to watch an animal be killed, or de-feathered or skinned.

Dad had two mules he used to pull the plow and till the soil for our spacious garden. Thinking back, I believe their names were "Buck" and "Red". Perhaps the reason these names come to mind, is my father "Buck" and his brother "Red" were as stubborn as these two mules.

I recall walking across the hill to special neighbors' home, Gladys and DeWitt Campbell, close friends of my father. We would enjoy fried chicken, gravy and biscuits. Sometimes, cake and peaches were served for Sunday lunch! It is nice to look back at all of us playing in the yard following lunch, enjoying the pleasures we had at no cost.

**Mill and Store with Reverend Alden Cross 1839 – 1938**

The memories I will now describe come from times with my grandparents, and parents. Charles Henry Cross, and Elizabeth Margaret Vaughn Cross. I was named Elizabeth in honor of both my grandmothers. My mother's parents were Bernard Sevier Easterly, and Elizabeth Kathrine "Kate" Bausel Easterly.

Grandpa "Bernie" owned the Old Mill where our school bus stop was located. We walked a mile or more to and from the home place back into the hollow. We never knew what to expect because Grandpa Bernie was a very outspoken Democrat.

Before television was invented, we'd often listen to the old Fibber McGee and Molly program on the radio, but being outside was our pleasure. I fondly recall visiting my grandparents and the joys of their big yard. There was a large apple tree which we would climb, and eat apples while sitting on the limbs. They had a big pond with colorful fish and a summer house with climbing roses on wooden poles.

How well I remember the cold water we carried from the "spring house". Grandmother would keep the butter and milk there because there was no electricity at that time. Everyone used oil lamps inside and lanterns outside. All of us had "outhouses", and the joke of a Sears and Roebuck Catalog in the outhouse was an actuality for all of us. I can recall tearing the pages!

Christmas gifts in the country were bought from selling tobacco crops, vegetables, and dairy products. I recall one year when dad did not make the tobacco sale until after Christmas. He had always bought a doll for me, but that year, my gift was a pretty set of tin dishes. He told me, "This will have to do until the tobacco sells". I cherished those dishes.

I realized later, it wasn't the best he wanted to do, but it was the best he could do that year. I saw his precious heart and sacrifice in my gift. I still love pretty dishes and enjoy cooking and displaying food on them. This is a pleasure and hobby of mine to this day. Christmas was an exciting time for us.

My sister, Patricia, had a great imagination. One year, one Christmas Eve, she declared she had seen Santa and seven reindeer. It was the year I had decided there was no Santa, so I announced to my mother, "There was no way Pat saw Santa and the reindeer". Pat said, "Mother, I did, I did". Mother didn't want to take away her happiness of still "believing in Santa", and replied to me, "Well, maybe, she did now". Pictured below, is my mother at one year of age.

*A Baby Girl Was Born*

**Charles Henry Cross**
**1871 – 1949**

**Margaret Elizabeth Cross**
**1880 – 1962**

**Bernard Sevier Easterly**
**1890 – 1967**

**Katherine Elizabeth Cross**
**1894 – 1965**

Fall pleasures included picking hickory nuts from the trees. My mother worked as a seamstress in a sewing factory before she married. I can remember watching her sew my clothes, pillow cases, making quilts, and washing them on a wash board. Later, we had an old ringer type washing machine. Regardless of the utilities she had, her work was immaculate, and she insisted on cleanliness. She would bathe us before dad would take us to visit our aunt at her store.

Aunt Tiny had an African American maid who offered to fix me something to eat. I noticed her hands were dark, and I asked her to wash them before giving me a piece of candy. My aunt and father told me repeatedly, "Look, look, she has thoroughly washed her hands". My fear came from my mother who had taught us that cleanliness was next to godliness. I have never had prejudice. Some of my greatest friends attend Shiloh Baptist Church. I enjoyed and appreciated them coming to sing for my birthdays and attending their church.

**Fanny "Wood" Cross**
**1912 – 2003**

**William "Buck" Cross**
**1909 – 1987**

# "My family, and the world changed"

## Chapter 2

My brother Charles was the second born, and I always felt protective of him. I often tried to keep him from falling in the fish pond. Many times he fell in, despite my efforts. I had to dry his little overalls beside a wood-burning stove. He would always get a spanking, and I would cry.

I recall my brother, Charles, and I going to trade at the Russell County Country Store. Mother sent hen eggs which we exchanged for flour, sugar, and other items. Usually we'd have 5 cents each remaining to purchase two candy bars for Charles and me. Mother, I'm sure, planned it that way.

The flour we purchased came in sacks, which was the material mother used to make our clothes. Our visitation with friends, admiration of nature and wildlife, and trips to the old country store meant more to us than movies and pricy venues that people are consumed by today.

Charles and I were very close. He was a handsome and quiet young man. Many called him "Little Pat Boone". He was thirty-nine when he was accidentally killed by a rock slide in the coal mines. He accepted Christ a few years before his death.

**Charles William Cross**

My sister, Patricia Sue was the third child in the family. By this time, mother let loose of "the reins" and said, "Whatever will be, will be!" At home, the children would run free, but at my grandparents' home, tight reins were still held. They taught us good manners and expected us to use them. Although they were lenient with me, sometimes I played sick in order to play hooky from school. I went to

swing from an old tire hanging from a tree. My brother Donald Gene Cross was the fourth child, and the last was Dema Faye Cross.

In the 1940's I recall my grandmother, "Kate", crying. It was the beginning of World War II, and her son, my "Uncle Bill", was inducted into the Army. Shortly thereafter, he was captured and became a prisoner of war. He was later released from captivity, and returned home following the end of the war. He had received a Purple Heart while in service, but it was sent to his mother. Following his death years later, his wife received the Normandy Award, in his honor. He'd received other awards during his life, and was a very talented musician.

I recall, as a young girl, enjoying him play the violin while I strummed a guitar. My aunts and uncles played together while my siblings and I thoroughly enjoyed the quite life in the country. We didn't realize grandmother Kate's "cry" was an emotion felt around the world, and would change our world as we knew it. Mother and dad would soon be taking five children out of the hills of Southwest Virginia to the City of Kingsport, Tennessee. Dad had taken a job at Holston Defense.

We had a difficult time adjusting to our new environment. We'd walk miles in the country and never get lost, but easily lost our way in the city.

Our first neighbors were Alberta and Wayne Ketron, parents of Wallace Ketron. Wallace, in later years, served as one of the Superintendents of Sullivan County Schools. We would often ride to school with Alberta, his mother. It was a difficult adjustment for us, especially for my mother, moving to the city and raising five children.

She was determined to involve us in community activities. Girl Scouts was my favorite. Our troop met at the old Stone Drive United Methodist Church. We roasted marshmallows under an old willow tree, which later would become the backyard where I raised my youngest son, Jantry, who I will later describe as a "special gift".

**Pictured above are Wallace Ketron and me, years later, at the Kingsport Senior Center.**

We attended Andrew Jackson Elementary School, and liked it very much. In sixth grade, we had graduation exercises, at John Sevier Junior High. It was my time to go back to Virginia to Lebanon High School, as our family was moving back to the country, following the war.

After the move back to the country, we became acquainted with new friends. I enjoyed playing basketball, and we would go to many games. Some fond memories of my siblings, during this time, are as follows: My sister, Faye, would always leave the dinner table early to go to choir practice. Even today, she sings in the choir, and is extremely active in her church.

My brother, Don, played the tuba in the band, and took Home Economics where he learned to cook. He still enjoys cooking, and I have one of his cookie recipes from his Lebanon High School class. My sister, Pat, was a majorette in the band, and later took piano lessons. My brother, Charles played tennis and enjoyed fishing and hunting. My parents took us to our various activities, and believed in having a social life.

My dad was a town policeman. He often hunted, and occasionally took me along. He was involved in public service, and remained deeply interested in politics. People seeking political positions sought his assistance. One person drove up the driveway, in an old Volkswagen, and asked my dad to help him run for Congress. Rick Boucher would, in later years, leave an enormous legacy. His hard work in Washington D.C. attributed to the prosperity in many areas of Southwest, Virginia.

He stated in a letter, he wrote to me, on March 14, 2006, that my dad had been one of his earliest friends, and a source of advice and encouragement. The framed letter hangs in my bedroom today, because I am proud of dad's wisdom to believe in a qualified young man who become the recognized Congressman Rick Boucher.

Mother was the homemaker of the family, and a wonderful cook. She made her lemon pies with fresh squeezed lemon juice. They were delicious! She had a green thumb and always had beautiful flowers year -round. In the winter months, she would sew, knit, and crochet. I still have some of her handiwork today.

Mother was always "well dressed", even if she was only going to the mailbox. She and dad enjoyed playing Rook with their closest friends, Hunter and Lillian Perry. Hunter was the local "Game Warden" and Lillian was a homemaker with a personality much like mothers.

Pictured here is my mother "Fanny Woodrow Easterly Cross" and me. My mother was upset for years having been named after President Woodrow Wilson, and despised the name "Fanny". In later years she was teased, and her friends began calling her "Woody". She and dad, from this time forward, were addressed as "Buck" and "Woody"

# "From the frying pan, into the fire"

## Chapter 3

At the age of fifteen, as the ole cliché goes, I "stepped out of the frying pan and into the fire". I was thinking I would have a wonderful life because I'd always been a dreamer. I left home and eloped on January 1, 1947, not knowing what would lie ahead. I was too young to be wed. Many in the family were displeased and were hoping to annul the marriage. I remained married and had three children. My first child was a little girl, born over a year later in Russell County, Virginia. Her birth was noted in the Russell County Newspaper, having been welcomed into the world by eight grandmothers. She was a special daughter.

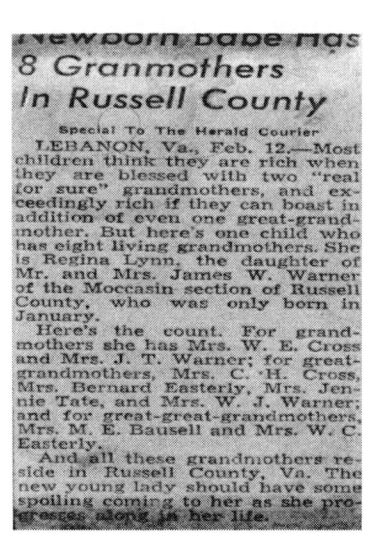

> **Newborn babe has 8 Granmothers In Russell County**
>
> Special To The Herald Courier
>
> LEBANON, Va., Feb. 12.—Most children think they are rich when they are blessed with two "real for sure" grandmothers, and exceedingly rich if they can boast in addition of even one great-grandmother. But here's one child who has eight living grandmothers. She is Regina Lynn, the daughter of Mr. and Mrs. James W. Warner of the Moccasin section of Russell County, who was only born in January.
>
> Here's the count. For grandmothers she has Mrs. W. E. Cross and Mrs. J. T. Warner; for great-grandmothers, Mrs. C. H. Cross, Mrs. Bernard Easterly, Mrs. Jennie Tate, and Mrs. W. J. Warner; and for great-great-grandmothers, Mrs. M. E. Bausell and Mrs. W. C. Easterly.
>
> And all these grandmothers reside in Russell County, Va. The new young lady should have some spoiling coming to her as she progresses along in her life.

**Pictured at (Left) are my husband Jim Warner and our first born daughter is pictured at (Right)**

I was a young mother, and it was exciting having a daughter. Being married had its challenges. Jim and I had some good times, but I was more of a servant to him and his family than a spouse. I felt obligated to do what all of them wanted instead of fulfilling my hopes and dreams.

One of my dreams was to become a model as my mother had hoped I would be. I was taking swimming lessons with a group at Legion Pool in Kingsport, and a modeling agency from New York was in town scouting for models. I was offered a contract with the company and was asked to move to New York.

**Me as a young mother**

At that time, I weighed 138 lbs. and was 5 feet and 8 inches tall. The timing and my responsibilities prevented me from taking this big step. As my daughter, Jeannie became a young lady, I spent my time supporting her endeavors and grooming her modeling potential. She later became a model for the J.C. Penny Company, while in high school, and did well.

**My Modeling Days**

*A Sentimental Journey*

JEAN WARNER welcomes the rain in her white with black polka dots trench coat. An extra precaution is the white leather boots.

Photo from the Kingsport Times News Sunday Edition on August 28, 1966. Photo was taken at the home built for Eastman President, Mr. J.C. White. It would later be the residence of J. Lane Latimer and family, founders of Oak Hill Funeral Home. My son, Jantry, now serves as General Manager of Oak Hill, and is an Alderman on the Kingsport BMA.

**Jeannie did well in school. She made the National BETA Club, and would later work for Congressman James H. "Jimmy" Quillen.**

She was in many beauty pageants, including the Miss Kingsport. One of her best friends and her tied for Miss Congeniality. During this contest, I joined Jeannie with the other contestants for a "Mothers' and Daughters' Tea" at the home of Mrs. J. Fred Johnson on Watauga Street. Mr. J. Fred Johnson was one of the founders of Kingsport.

"Oh, no, not again"
Regina Warner

Mike Warner is going to school. (Left). Optimist Club Pee Wee League is featured in the Kingsport Times News on Sunday, September 11, 1960 (Right). He joined the Army Reserves, and was employed by Eastman. He graduated from Tusculam College. I was so proud of him! He also worked overseas for Eastman Chemical Company.

My third child, Steve Warner and I are having fun in the sun! He loved sports and fishing. He began driving a truck for Air Products, and later became the General Manager until his sudden death. He was well loved by all and coached many ball teams. I last saw him on a Christmas Eve, a few years ago. He hugged and kissed me, and told

Jantry how proud he was of him. It was the best Christmas gift!

Jeannie graduated from East Tennessee State University. She went to work for Congressman Jimmy Quillen, at the 1$^{st}$ District office in downtown Kingsport, where the post office is on Center Street. She had majored in English, and was well qualified for this position.

Jimmy later moved Jeannie to his Washington office as his personal secretary. I was working at a lady's dress shop in downtown Kingsport, and would go to Washington every chance I had. I loved everything about it, except the flight!

# "Unexpected Changes"
## Chapter 4

**Lordy, Lordy, I Turned Forty**     **Someone New... I was 42**

When I was 42 years old, I had an unexpected gift. My last child, Jantry, was born in 1974. His birth brought big changes into my life! I accepted him with joy!

~ 21 ~

## A Sentimental Journey

My second husband had worked for the Government in Washington D.C.. He moved to Kingsport and opened a jewelry store. I went to help him some, and one day he asked me to go look at a house he'd found. When I arrived at the address, I was pleasantly surprised. The very willow tree I sat under in the scouts was in the backyard. We bought the home. We met wonderful and caring neighbors who were friends throughout the years.

Reverend Dewey Ramey and his lovely wife Margaret are pictured at left. Pictured at right, is my old back yard which held the Willow Tree years ago where I roasted marshmallows. The old Stone Drive United Methodist Church lot, and the fence where Jantry would climb and yell "hello preacher" has become the location for a Walgreens store in Kingsport! Many changes have taken place in 80 years!

Jantry began at Andrew Jackson Elementary and joined the scouts as I had as a child. It brought back many memories

## Unexpected Changes

of my childhood days in Kingsport. When he was in the second grade at Jackson, my husband died unexpectedly. It was a tragic time! I was fifty, a single parent, and it was a scary time in my life.

My other children had their own families, though they helped me as they could. His scout troop and school friends were a big support for him during these times. One day a knock came on my door. It was Preacher Mike Stout from the church up the street, offering an invitation. We began to attend and nearly a year later, Jantry accepted the Lord, which I had done years before. I had not always made the right choices and was deeply regretful.

On a Sunday morning, I rededicated my life, and Jantry and I were baptized together. We joined West View Baptist Church where we are members today. I couldn't have made it through many difficult times, if it hadn't been for the Lord, my church family, and friends. As time went on, I became content and more encouraged. I was working at the Family Dollar Store, downtown. My friend, Mae Cook, who worked at First Broad Street United Methodist Church asked if I wanted to help her in the kitchen. She was the head cook.

I began working at First Broad Street as a second job. It was a totally different environment. At Family Dollar, I was the head cashier and retail was not easy, especially during busy holiday seasons. It became harder stocking and maintaining the store, but I did it. Two or three days each week I would work at the church helping prepare for receptions and dinners. I had never worked in a commercial kitchen before, so I had some learning to do. My friend, Mae, was the head cook, and we had many laughs in my learning process. One day while whipping potatoes in a huge mixer, I got a long spoon stuck in the mixer, and potatoes went flying to the ceiling and everywhere. I yelled , "Oh, what shall I do? "Oh, what shall I do?". Mae replied, in the midst of her laughing, "turn the mixer off first!"

I later learned many special recipes that I still use during holidays. Everyone teased me about having to replace the mangled spoon. Thank goodness it was a joke. I could not even make ends meet with the two jobs while raising a child. I met so many friends at First Broad Street.

They were like a second church family and helped me so much with Jantry. It was a blessing that Jantry was in scouts there. Dr. Tombs Kay was the senior minister at the time and worked with him to get his "God and Country Award" in the Boy Scouts. I met Terry Kay, Tomb's brother, who was the author of "To Dance With The White Dog". He autographed the book for me. The book was made into a movie which was later shown on the Hallmark Channel. I received a copy of the movie, and my mother and I watched it together. It was one of our favorites along with "Driving Miss Daisy". I was inspired by so many people there. Jantry was involved in many things, so I had to have more income. I began to go to the School for Practical Nursing. It was a choice that became a ministry!

**My retirement lunch from First Broad Street UMC**

**Mother and Fathers Golden Anniversary**

My parents were a great encouragement in my life. Even though they remained in Russell County, VA, I always knew they were there for me. By this time I was working three jobs and in my mid-fifties. I was a dedicated and hard worker. My third job was beginning my nursing school clinical at Hillside Manor Nursing Home. School was taking every spare moment I had.

I later left the Family Dollar Store and would eventually retire from my work at First Broad Street Church, following graduation from nursing school. Looking back, I have no idea how I did it, but I did. Jantry rarely missed his activities in scouts, church, theater, sports, orchestra, and other activities. I am thankful for the friends and family who assisted me. I graduated at the top of my class, and began a career in healthcare attending to patients needs until I was age 75. It was not always easy, but it was a rewarding experience to care for those who could not care for themselves.

# "Life and death experiences"
## Chapter 5

**Jeannie and I in Richmond, VA**  **Jeannie and her grandmother**

(Above right) is the Warner family, in a public park, in Church Hill, TN. They are a large family who have all accomplished a great deal, and stay busy with their responsibilities and enjoying their lives. Though Jeannie has been away for years, she and I have visited often. While Jeannie was working for Congressman Quillen, she met her husband and they later moved to Richmond, VA where I would visit them as often as possible. Her husband was always a comedian, and we never had a dull moment. We are pictured below in a comical pose at Bush Gardens in Williamsburg, VA., with my mother.

Now with just one job, and Jantry getting older, I had more time to visit with my parents. My dad was not well and was in and out of Indian Path Medical Center during his last years. In between working, I would go sit with him. He would always enjoy watching the sun set outside his window, and would admire it's beauty. He went home to Heaven, and my mother would live alone at the home place in Russell County, Virginia, until past the age of ninety. I would visit her as often as I could. My sisters and I would stay many nights with her.

In high school, Jantry took a part-time job at the Kingsport Veterinary Hospital, and later while a sophomore at Dobyns-Bennett High School went to work part-time at Oak Hill Funeral Home and Cemetery. The cemetery was where Jeannie had learned to drive, and I taught Jantry to drive there also. Following his high school graduation, he would eventually go on to funeral college at John A. Gupton College in Nashville, TN. Frequently he managed his time to take me to visit mother and take us on little trips. We went to Pigeon Forge, and often just for rides through the country. Mother and I were very close. There is no one like a mother, and she was special!

*Life And Death Experiences*

Students, after graduation, take some time to find the proper career. After a few years, Jantry found his vocation and life calling at Oak Hill Funeral Home. We were excited for him. My sisters, and sweet mother came to visit, and we are pictured with Naomi Hamilton, Wayne's wife (Right). They were just like family to us. Wayne was like a father to Jantry and helped him through a lot during his early years. He had attended the same funeral college years before.

*A Sentimental Journey*

While Jantry was in Nashville, Wayne encouraged him. I would meet Ms. Ann Garrett, who's husband started the funeral home where Jantry lived. She is a wonderful lady, and we remain in touch . Jantry enjoyed driving her to church and house-sitting often.

Wayne and Naomi were like family, and I would bake them cornbread. Wayne loved my cornbread. They belonged to a hot air balloon team and during Fun Fest in 2001 they had taken Jantry up with them during the balloon race. Moments after the balloon landed, Wayne dropped dead of a major heart attack. It was a shocking tragedy for the entire community. Later the chapel at Oak Hill was named the J. Wayne Hamilton Memorial Chapel.

A few years later, following the death of Wayne Hamilton Jantry received the "Forty under 40 Award" presented by "The Business Journal of Tri-Cities/Southwest Virginia" Wayne was looking down on us with his smile that day. Jantry was later made manager of Oak Hill Funeral Home.

# "Turning (70) and going strong"
## Chapter 6

**Headed to work at the nursing home in my BMW**

I was nearing (70) years old, and Jantry was determined to make me happy and keep me safe. I had sacrificed throughout the years for him, and he hasn't forgotten. He had bought me several cars, and the last one I would ever drive was a big BMW 740il. It was my favorite, of course. I had come a long way from riding a mule in the "hollow!" My aunt Aggie never drove, and I loved picking her up and going places. She meant so much to me, and was a strong source of comfort to me during many difficult times.

*A Sentimental Journey*

We loved to laugh and have fun. She was a down-to-earth lady, and wasn't that fond of "uppity people". In her later years, after my mother died, Jantry joined the country club, and I insisted we have a special birthday party for Aunt Aggie. She couldn't stand the thought of going the the country club. Once she got there, it was a different story. She loved it! It was one of the "highlights of her life" she told me.

Aggie and I always joked a lot. After I turned (70), Jantry wanted me to go on his company trips with him. Aunt Aggie said, "Go... while you can". Stewart Enterprises, Inc. was full of so many wonderful people who became like our family. They still keep in touch with us from across the country. Pictured above are my "big fun glasses" for I would be traveling more than ever before!

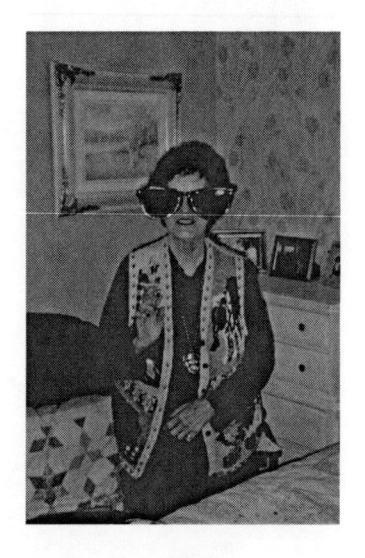

**Sitting on the dock in Tybee Island, Georgia**

I had the privilege of meeting Mr. Frank Stewart, who began Stewart Enterprises, Inc. His company bought Oak Hill Funeral Home and Cemetery, and the Cole and Garrett Funeral Home, in Nashville, where Jantry worked as a student in funeral college. Mr. Stewart was an amazing, down-to-earth gentleman. I recall him talking about death being like "blowing a candle out and walking into the bright sunlight". He is very religious. It is a wonderful company, and I have met interesting people in my travels with Jantry to his meetings. This was in Tampa, Florida, in 2007 at Saddle Brook Resort. It was a lovely place and very relaxing. I could have stayed forever!

*A Sentimental Journey*

I'm standing at the Fountain of Youth in St. Augustine. It rained so hard, I had to wear a poncho. I said, "It would be my luck to drown at the Fountain of Youth!".

Charleston, South Carolina was one of the most beautiful cities. I rode the horse and buggy through the old town, and ate at "High Cotton!".

# "Retiring Alive at (75)"

## Chapter 7

After serving at the nursing home for nearly twenty years, and turning (75), it was time to retire. I was shocked at my 75$^{th}$ Surprise Birthday when the President of Sunbridge Nursing Home presented me with a retirement plaque. The Mayor of Kingsport also presented a proclamation naming the day in my honor!

Being retired was a weird feeling, at first, following (75) years of hard work. It didn't take me long to get used to it. I finally began to enjoy so many things I had never been able to do!

I won the "Keep Kingsport Beautiful" Beautification Award in 2002. I was so excited when I went out to look, I locked myself out and was in my pink house shoes. Jantry and Tom Taylor were having lunch, and stopped by to let me in the house. Tom couldn't resist a teasing photo.

I loved a neat yard with many pretty flowers, but never had the time to sit and enjoy it until now. I had a deck built years ago when Jantry was younger because the traffic was so dangerous in front our home. It deteriorated over the years, and the insects "would eat us alive". I was hoping one day to have a sunroom like my mother and dad had in the country. Little did I know at the time, what was around the corner. Another surprise awaited me!

Fun Fest was always a treat! I met Gavin Degraw! (Above); and Kimberly Locke is pictured below. I loved their music and they were very nice people.

Through my working years, many times I could not afford to take a vacation. I would go on a day or weekend trip to Pigeon Forge. A year or more after I retired, Jantry surprised me with a gift of a timeshare, at a condo there. I loved it, and went there about four or five times each year until recently. I can't travel the distance anymore. We met some talented gentlemen who play music for Dolly Parton. They became close friends. I also made friends with the resort Parrot, who ironically was named "Fanny", like my mother's first name.

**Relaxing times at my little "home away from home" in Pigeon Forge, TN**

My 77th Surprise Birthday Party was the beginning of a new, and wonderful friendship. Jantry's friends, Bill Young from Dixie Stampede, and Gary Davis who had been Dolly Parton's band manager, came to the condo and surprised my sisters and me!

My two sisters are with me at the Dixie Stampede for my 77th Birthday Surprise! Complimentary tickets were provided to us all with special seating by Dolly!

*A Sentimental Journey*

I enjoyed attending many campaign events, community functions, chamber dinners and churches. Helen Doty and I enjoyed being with the Marines at a Memorial Day celebration at Oak Hill Funeral Home. The opening of the Kingsport Higher Education Center was a highlight of my experiences. Mr. Pal Barger and I are pictured at bottom (left) at my son's election victory. Mr. Barger contributed significantly to the Kingsport Higher Education Initiative as evidenced by the Pal Barger School of Automotive Technology. The project gained an award from Harvard!

## The trip I said I would never take, was the trip of my lifetime! New Orleans here I come!

## A Sentimental Journey

On the way to NOLA, we stayed at the famous Tuttwiler Hotel in Burmingham, AL. When in NOLA, we toured Burbon Street. I loved the Jazz music. We passed the Super Dome, ate lunch at Emeril's, played at Harrah's, and stopped on the way back in beautiful Tybee Island, GA.

## Little did I know what would await me when I returned!

Jantry, my dear friend Barbara Brown, and others were fulfilling my wish for a sunroom. My dream became a reality! When we pulled in the back driveway, I thought I was at some other home! I could not believe my eyes! I enjoyed it for several years before moving to my present home. My sister Pat and I exited the car, and stood there in amazement. We could not believe what we were seeing!. Jantry secretly planned all this for me while in NOLA. My daughter, her daughter, and grandson, enjoyed it with us several times. It reminded us of my parents sunroom!

I had the honor of visiting the Latimer's at their new home in Linville Ridge, NC. They owned the home Jeannie was pictured at in Kingsport, and founded Oak Hill. They are some of the kindest and most interesting people I have met.

# "Slowing Down, But Not Stopping"
## Chapter 8

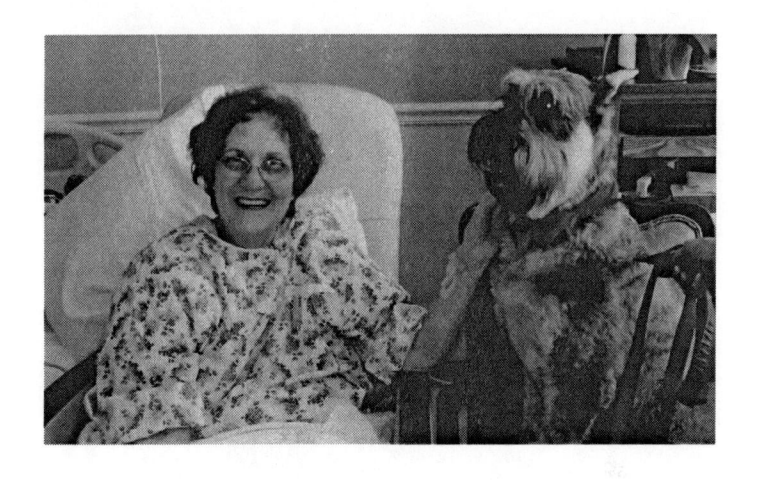

Even in the hospital, my son and some friends gave me wonderful surprises. Jantry sent a therapy dog to visit some when I was depressed. Her name was "Louise". My wonderful longtime friends, Wanda and Brian have always made sure that my life was happier and more comfortable. Wanda and I worked together, in the nursing home for many years, and shared laughter and tears. My good friend Helen Doty has always been a true friend and wonderful support.

*A Sentimental Journey*

**Wanda and Me**

After the hospital recovery in 2009, that fall I was ready to travel again. Pat and I were taken in a motor home to Richmond, VA to visit my daughter and her family. It was the most scenic fall trip I'd every taken. The relaxing motor home had big windows and was so roomy. We stopped and ate at the Natural Bridge, which was my halfway point, when I would drive to visit Jeannie through the years.

**Biltmore, The Oak Park in the Mountains, The Red Hats, and Water Falls.**

"From the circus to the zoo, and a stop at Ridgewood Barbecue".

A butterfly landed on my head at the zoo. I "dipped my wick" at Rocky Mt., to make a wax candle, as they did in the 1800's. We visited with a good friend Ms. Ann Garrett in Nashville. Staying active was my choice, rather than growing old, lying in the bed, and covering up my head!

## Slowing Down, But Not Stopping

I was sitting at home, when I turned (79), and "low and behold", friends and family gave me a big surprise. The Shiloh Choir came to sing, and my dear friend, Bill Young, came up from Pigeon Forge to perform in my home. I had always wished that all my friends could meet and hear Bill and Gary who visited and played at our condo in the mountains. Bill made it happen. I wish Gary Davis could have been there also, but I would live to experience another surprise. Approximately (70) friends and family came to wish me a wonderful birthday, and it was great!

### THE ROAD HOME

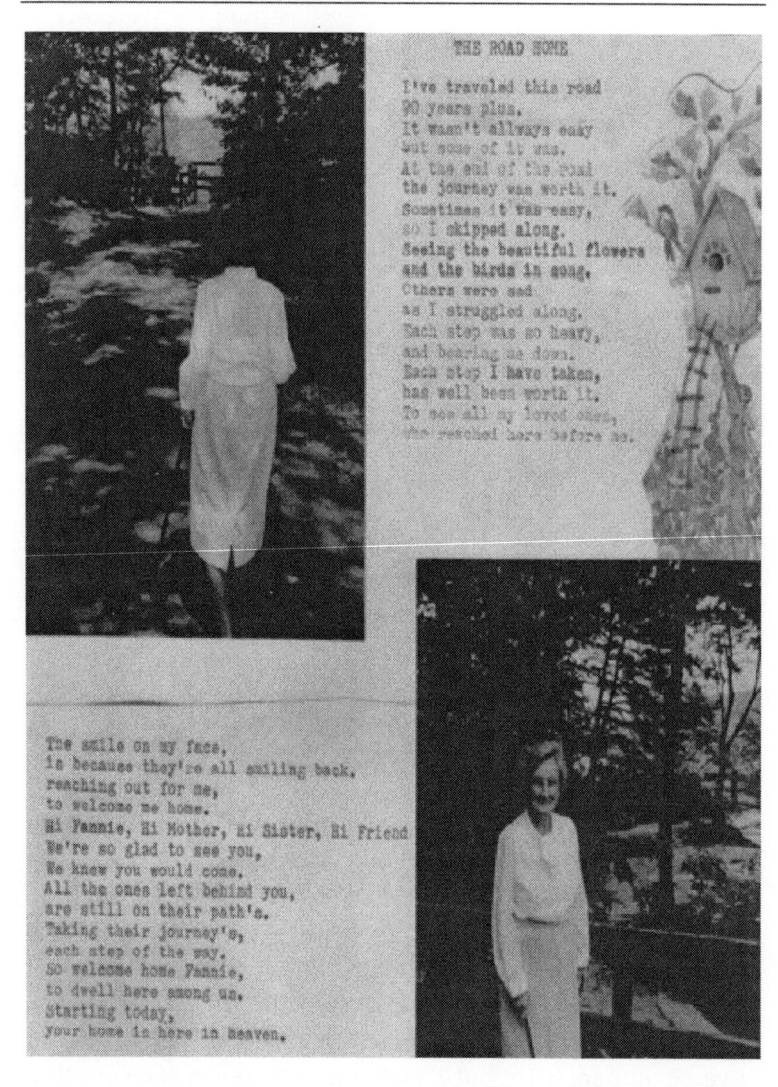

I've traveled this road
90 years plus.
It wasn't allways easy
but some of it was.
At the end of the road
the journey was worth it.
Sometimes it was easy,
so I skipped along.
Seeing the beautiful flowers
and the birds in song.
Others were sad
as I struggled along.
Each step was so heavy,
and bearing us down.
Each step I have taken,
has well been worth it.
To see all my loved ones,
who reached here before us.

The smile on my face,
is because they're all smiling back,
reaching out for me,
to welcome me home.
Hi Fannie, Hi Mother, Hi Sister, Hi Friend
We're so glad to see you,
We knew you would come.
All the ones left behind you,
are still on their path's.
Taking their journey's,
each step of the way.
So welcome home Fannie,
to dwell here among us.
Starting today,
your home is here in heaven.

Closer to Heaven than here, this poem, "The Road Home" is so meaningful to me. It was written by my brother Don's wife, Myrtle, in honor of my mother when she passed away.

From taking my aunt Aggie places, to helping my mother with her flowers, I have begun to experience what I never understood years ago. It is hard to give up my independence and rely on others for my daily needs.

I had the determination to keep on helping others, for a while, as long as I was able. After moving, I started a Ceramic Class at Crown Cypress Assisted Living. Following another stay in the hospital, I realized that I could no longer participate in the class. I'm thankful someone else is continuing what I started. The residents were excited about talent they didn't realize they had.

*Slowing Down, But Not Stopping*

# (80), Alive, and again.... surprised!

**My close friends and I in the limo ride of a lifetime!**

**Congressman Phil Roe and me!**

*A Sentimental Journey*

I had several birthday parties in my days, but this was the best of all! Dolly Parton sends another surprise!

Queen of the Red Hats and myself

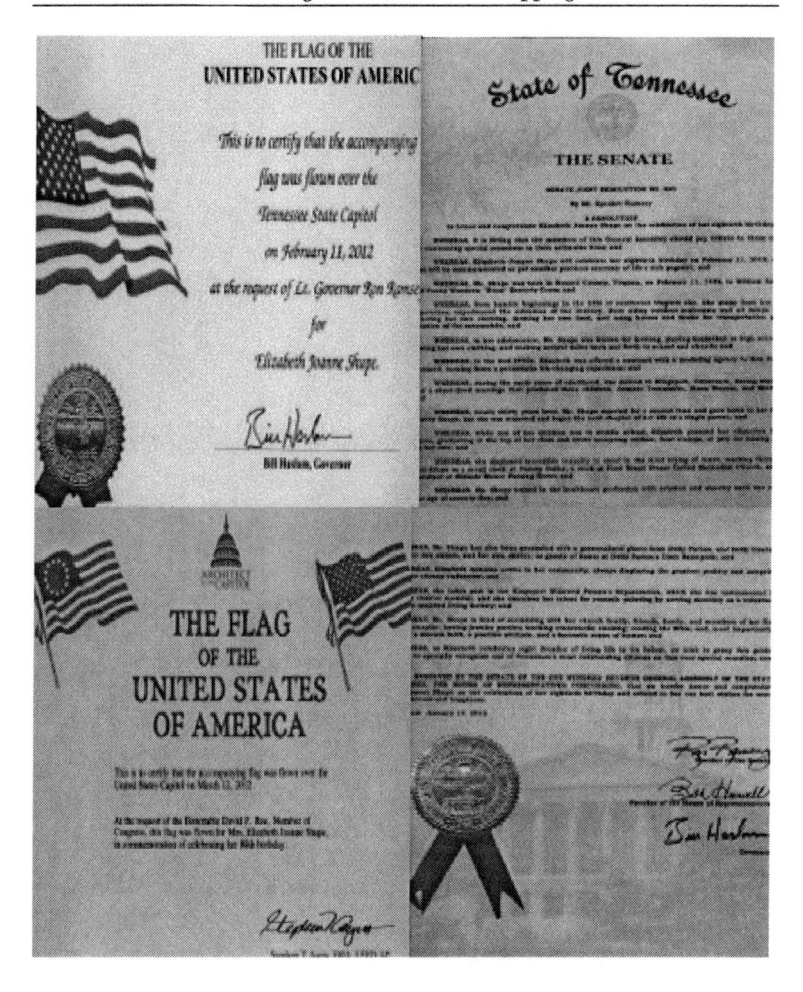

The American Flag was flown over the Tennessee State Capitol, and the United States Capitol in honor of my 80$^{th}$ Birthday. I was presented with a special resolution from the Tennessee State Senate, and entered into the Congressional Record. I felt very humbled and honored!

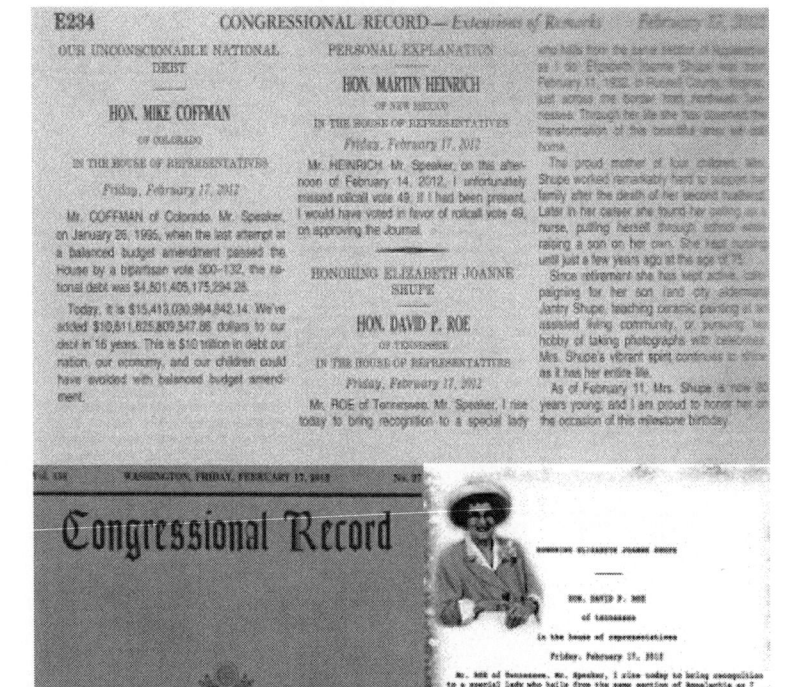

**Bill Young, Gary Davis, and Congressman Roe play and sing to a hundred or more friends and family on a snowy, but delightful 80th Surprise Birthday Party!!! It topped them all!!!**

## Slowing Down, But Not Stopping

On the front cover of my book titled, "A Sentimental Journey". The background was me standing by the "ole hollow" where I was born and raised. The name of the road leading to our homeplace is pictured there.

### "Buck Cross Road"

I want to direct your attention, in my closing remarks, to this road named after my father, where my journey began.. He taught me that no one is perfect, but everyone can leave a legacy of helping others. They can be remembered long after they're gone. He loved to plant seeds and watch them grow, but it was not just his garden he planted seeds in. It was in many lives, including mine. Today, I am 80 years young, and looking back. I hope that I've have planted some good seeds that will make many lives better. I certainly have done my best.

In closing, I wish family, friends, and anyone who may read my life story, a successful life, and love always. I wish that ten percent of any book proceeds will go to a college fund for single parent nursing students. I know from experience, that any financial assistance a single parent can get is appreciated. The healthcare field is a mission field, needing caring people, especially in nursing homes. It was my greatest calling, and the best seed I could ever plant. Thank you for reading my story. I have enjoyed my journey, thus far, and the many blessings of life along the way. God bless you.

Sincerely,<br>Elizabeth J. Shupe

CPSIA information can be obtained at www.ICGtesting.com
Printed in the USA
LVOW041202010912

296907LV00001B/7/P

9 781432 797423